Three Baby Butterflies

Dayton Kennedy Roche   **July 28, 2008**

Dakota Kaitlyn Roche   **July 28, 2008**

Damaria Kenyette Roche   **July 27, 2008**

Three Baby Butterflies
Toniqua Davis
Copyright © 2009 Toniqua Davis
Cover Image by Digital Vision / Getty Images
ISBN 978-0-578-02040-2

Table Of Contents

Three Baby Butterflies

This book is about the joy and anticipation I felt about being pregnant with triplet girls. I have two sons, and am currently pregnant with son number three. I carried my sweet babies for twenty-two weeks, just long enough for them to be considered stillbirths, but not long enough for them to be considered viable enough for life saving procedures. The gestational age for fetuses to be considered viable is twenty-four weeks. My precious babies were just two weeks away from even being given the consideration to live. I have spoken to medical professionals who have assured me that even though twenty-four weeks is considered the age of viability, my daughters may have eventually died anyway, or suffered from long term disabilities. I have done research and found some very rare cases of very early premature babies that were given life saving treatment at twenty-two weeks gestation and survived with very mild complications. The cases were rare, but I would have given anything to see my daughters given that chance. I am however, grateful for the short time I was able to hold and love my only daughters. May you rest in peace sweet babies.

Chapter One
February-Conception

My fiancé and I were going through the regular ups and downs of most couples who have been together for years. We were planning on getting married some time this year. In preparation for the marriage the issue of having children together came up. We discussed whether or not we were going to have children off and on. I figured since we were going to get married this year, combined with the fact that we both were both kind of old, me two months away from turning thirty-five, and he just shy of forty, that we should get started. I read that once a woman becomes thirty-five she becomes "high risk." Besides, I figured it would take a couple of months for "it" to happen, since I was currently taking the pill. I told my fiancé in January that I was going to stop taking the pill this month. He did not agree with, nor contest my decision, so as far as I was concerned, it was a go.

I had two teenaged sons already. However, I figured I should at least have one child by my husband. He had children from previous relationships as well, but they were grown, with the exception of one. Prior to my startling revelation about discontinuing my birth control, we had conversations about having a daughter. I thought it would be a refreshing change to have a girl in the house. I could buy pink this and that, dresses, and all sorts of frilly girly things. My family thought I was insane for wanting to start all over again. If were to conceive this year I would have a newborn, a fourteen year old, and an eighteen year old. Hell, maybe I was insane. At any rate if it was going to happen there was no need to procrastinate. Time was of the essence.

Before I became totally committed to the idea of having another child I began watching those health shows on television that dealt with childbirth and newborns. I was particularly interested in shows that discussed pregnancy for women over the age of thirty-five. There were a few shows that followed the lives of "older" women undergoing a battery of test to detect chromosomal abnormalities. For the most part, the babies were healthy. There were women in their late thirties and early forties who were at high risk of having babies with Downs Syndrome, who had healthy babies. I became concerned about the possibility of having a child with disabilities, but the cases were rare and were not only confined to women in my age group. Once I put my mind at ease about the possible complications of pregnancy over thirty-five, I was ready.

I believe I took my last pill around the first of the month. The literature I read concerning conception after the pill was contradictory. It read that if you miss one pill you could become pregnant. It also read that if you take the pill consistently, it takes a few months to conceive. The way I looked at it, I could become pregnant a day or months after discontinuing the pill. Near the end of the month it seemed as if I became increasingly hormonal. I was having symptoms like it was time for my period, but I just had one two weeks prior. The slightest annoyance seemed to set me off. I was yelling and screaming so much about any and everything that I developed new veins in my neck and forehead. I was a very relaxed person prior to whatever ailment I was suffering from. I was basically the same, just a temper **"mental"** version of myself.

For the life of me I couldn't figure out why any and everything got on my last nerve. I figured that since it was a couple of weeks before my period that was the cause of my mood swings. I never really had mood swings before, but I was getting older and I know women's bodies go through changes as we age. March was fast approaching, so maybe the arrival of spring would help put me in a happier mood. The thought of the sun shining, flowers, birds singing, and …….oh hell, who am I kidding, all that shit would probably just get on my nerves! At any rate I will stop focusing on what is causing my temporary insanity and focus on preparing for the wedding that is scheduled to occur this summer. I have heard so many horror stories about wedding planning. The stress of getting married and having a blended family may be contributing to my madness. I wondered if I would get pregnant before the wedding and if so would I have to get a maternity wedding dress, or would the wedding be postponed. ARRRRRGH! The next few months will probably prove to be more mind altering than this one.

Chapter Two
March-Read Between the Lines

It's around the first week of March and for the life of me I cannot stop peeing. I don't think I have a bladder infection, but I seem to have to go to the bathroom every hour. I have increased my water intake, so that very well may be the culprit. I guess I need to make a doctor's appointment and stop worrying about it. I still seem a little crankier than usual, however, I have two teenaged sons and now an uncooperative bladder. I guess I am entitled to an outburst or twenty! I figured with all the talk of pregnancy and conception, I may have psyched myself out. I was not sick and I had not missed a period, so I figured it must be my nerves.

A couple of days passed and I started feeling a little bloated. I had just had a period, (though it was light), so I figured that was the reason behind my bloating. However, that did not explain the constant peeing. I did not have tender breast, or any other classic pregnancy symptoms, but I still did not quite feel like myself. I went on for a few more days and no change. I could not quite put a finger on what could be wrong with me, but I would eventually figure it out. I went on for a few more days and it seemed as if the bloating subsided, but the peeing remained constant. Would I have to buy some adult diapers? I figured after a week or so I would be fine, so I did not dwell on it so much (this week).

It is March tenth. Just for the sake of my own sanity I decided to purchase a home pregnancy test. I decided to get the one with two in the package in case of user error or in case it was too soon to detect the pregnancy. As soon as I got home, (of course I had to pee) I sat on the toilet rocking from side to side trying not to let go of one drop before I could get the damn wrapper off the test stick. Droplets of pee were trickling into the toilet, and I was finally able to free the stubborn test stick and hold it sideways into the stream of urine now pouring from my bladder. I sat the test stick on the sink's countertop and awaited the results. The instructions read that it took one minute for a positive result and three minutes for a negative result to register. The instructions also indicated that a "control'" line would appear first, then a results line (if the test was positive). I watched the "control" line appear in the test window and sat in awe for five minutes too see if a second line would appear. There was only one line. Oh well, I'm not pregnant after all. There must be some other explanation for my current craziness.

It was the end of March, the twenty-sixth, to be exact and I was preparing to take my mother out to dinner for her birthday. I got home from work around five o'clock and had two hours to get ready. At around five thirty I had to pee. I started to get the second test stick just for grins and giggles, but I decided if I had to pee again before I left, I would use it then. At six thirty, while on my way out the door, I had to pee again. I frantically grabbed the second test stick from my pregnancy test duo and followed the same instructions as last time. After placing the test stick on the countertop I didn't look at it until after I wiped and flushed. There was the "control" line again as it was before, but this time there was a faint line next to it. I sat back down on the toilet with the lid down, and just stared at the second line for what seemed to be hours (five minutes). I thought to myself, well I'll be damned! No wonder I was walking around here like a mad woman. I had just taken a test two weeks ago and it was negative. I had a period, although it was light. Was it too soon to detect the pregnancy then? When the hell did I get pregnant? I called my fiancé and told him the news. He was quiet for a moment and then asked me was I sure. I told him I could save the test until after dinner, but he decided it would be best if we got a fresh one. I asked him how did he feel about it and he told me that we would discuss that after dinner as well. I did not know if this was a good sign. I guess I will just have to wait until after dinner to find out.

The dinner was uneventful. I was so preoccupied with the "news" I almost could not focus on anything else. I made sure not to eat or drink anything that may be harmful to the baby. I sat through dinner like a zombie. After I gave my mom her gift, everything afterward was a blur. All I could think about was the teeny tiny life inside of me that I was unaware of until a few hours ago. After dinner my fiancé and I made a B-line to the pharmacy and purchased yet another home pregnancy test. I made sure we got the dual pack again, in case it needed to be redone. I read that it is ideal to use the first urine of the day, although I got a positive result in the evening. Soon as I got home, (yes I had to pee), I whipped out the test stick and held it under yet another urine stream. The instructions indicated that a positive result took one minute register. I could almost swear that the "control" line and its twin appeared across that stick in under thirty seconds flat! I showed the results to my skeptical fiancé and we stared at each other for an eternity (five minutes) without saying a word. Finally, my fiancé said "now what?" Good question.

The next morning I made an appointment with my OB/GYN to confirm that I was indeed pregnant and if so, how far along I was. My appointment was scheduled for April fourth, the day after my birthday. I was so preoccupied with the news of the pregnancy I did not even think about what I was I going to do, if anything for my birthday. I guess this is an early birthday present.

The following week flew by with rapid succession. My fiancé and I celebrated my cousin's birthday with her at a local bar/pool hall on March twenty-eighth. I did not drink anything and she did not question my lack of alcohol consumption. I figured it was too soon to tell anyone, besides, I was not certain if the test was accurate. We all laughed and joked our way through the evening and all was well. After we left the bar/pool hall I called my cousin and made sure she got to her destination okay and called it a night.

My fiancé and I returned to my apartment and discussed how and when we were going to break the news to everyone. I figured we needed to wait until the pregnancy was confirmed and I was aware of how many weeks I was. Although I had children already, I was very young then, and did not obsess over things as I did with this pregnancy. I felt that it would be best to tell everyone when I was about twelve weeks. At that time the risk of miscarriage drops drastically. I did not anticipate a miscarriage, but I was older and I had to be aware of certain risks that may not have been of concern with my previous children. My fiancé agreed and it was settled.

Soon it was the last day of the month and we were both anticipating the fourth. My hormones were a little more relaxed and I wasn't as crazy as I had been. I guess we will just have to wait and see what is in store for us next month. I am pretty sure I can keep my hormones and temperament under control for the time being. Now that I had a valid explanation for what was wrong with me, it seems that I had been a bit calmer and a tad more pleasant. I think I can keep this up. Until next month that is.

Chapter Three
April-Very Pregnant

My birthday flew by so fast I do not recall anything that occurred. The next day I went to my doctor's office optimistic and anxious. The doctor generally uses the same urine method as the home test. The only way to be 100% certain is by fetal ultrasound or by blood testing. I sat in the lobby and waited for my name to be called. "Just go to the restroom and leave a urine sample in one of the clear cups. Don't forget to write your name on the label," one of the nurses ordered. After I left my sample I was escorted to one of the patient rooms. I waited for about twenty minutes or so and the doctor appeared at last. "You are pregnant", she said. "Yes!" I thought to myself. "You are thirty-five, so there may be risks. I am going to refer you to Maternal Fetal Medicine." What! What the hell is she talking about? I see old broads, (though most of them are celebrities) having babies all the time. "I am going to schedule you for an ultrasound on the twelfth," she concluded. Well that's that. I am pregnant.

I called my fiancé and told him that not only was I indeed pregnant, I was also a pregnant fossil according to the doctor. He asked what the next step was and I told him about the ultrasound appointment. He agreed to accompany me and I thought to myself, "hell yeah you are coming". I simply told him that it was an excellent idea for him to come, since he was the accomplice in this matter. We chit chatted for a while then hung up. I went to sleep and dreamt about the tiny being inside me. It was the first time I slept peacefully since taking the pregnancy test. I was really looking forward to a new baby.

The next day, on April fifth, my fiancé threw a surprise birthday party for me. He invited only my closest friends and family. I was so excited. In the past, I usually had a party every five years, starting at age twenty. However, because of the pregnancy news I did not even think about planning a party for my thirty-fifth birthday. It was at a restaurant, so the kids were able to come. My friends, oblivious to my current "situation" were all offering to buy me drinks. "Not in front of the kids," I said. My kids were bigger than me and my fiancé. Couldn't I come up with a more valid excuse? After about three drink offers and refusals, no one questioned why I would not consume alcohol. It was still too early to tell people that I was pregnant. The evening was relaxed. Everyone had a good time. Only a few of my friends could not make it, but they called and wished me well. My dad said I looked a little plump in the face. I told him that my weight fluctuates sometimes and that was that.

At the conclusion of the evening, my cousin took the kids to her house and my fiancé and I had the night to ourselves. Once at his house, we briefly talked about our impending growing family. After the conversation, we went to sleep. I woke up feeling a little nauseous, so I went to the bathroom. I leaned over the toilet to vomit, but nothing came out. I used the bathroom, wiped myself and saw a few drops of blood. I knew this was not normal, so I woke up my fiancé. I called my doctor and informed her of the situation and she told me to go to the hospital. I decided to wait until morning to see if the bleeding would stop. The next morning there was fresh blood when I wiped. I went to the hospital.

While at the hospital the first thing they asked me was how far along in the pregnancy I was. I did not know, so an ultrasound was ordered. I had to wait for what seemed like an eternity to see a doctor. I was so glad my fiancé was there to keep me company. I would have been bored to death waiting alone. The doctor performed a pelvic exam to confirm that my cervix was closed. It was closed! He also wanted to see how much blood I was passing and if there was any tissue. There was no tissue and the blood was brown and minimal. He said that because the blood was brown, it was an indication that the blood was "old" and that he did not think I was at risk of having a miscarriage. That was good news!

Finally, I was whisked away to ultrasound. The ultrasound technician squeezed a very cold gel on my lower abdomen and starting moving the transducer back and forth. She could not get a clear reading, so she ultimately had to perform a transvaginal ultrasound. This is when they stick an eight inch probe into your vagina to get a clearer picture of the fetus if you are very early in your pregnancy. Once the probe was inserted, the technician asked me if I ever had fibroids or cysts. "No.", I replied. "Okay", she said with a puzzled look on her face. After everything was said and done, the doctor came in to speak to my fiancé and I. He said he believed that I was about five weeks pregnant and that he thought I might have a fibroid or cyst near the baby. I asked him was there a cause for concern, but he just simply said to follow up with my doctor. I called my doctor and she told me to keep my April twelfth appointment if there were no more complications.

The following week flew by, and it is now April twelfth. It seems that since my pregnancy has been confirmed, I have been nauseous every day. I am so excited that we get to see our tiny one up close for the first time. I am also concerned because of the "fibroid or cyst" near the baby. I am estimating that I am around five weeks or so based on the information given by the hospital and because I didn't get a positive pregnancy test until the end of March. However, I have been moody for the past seven weeks. We will find out for sure today exactly how far along I am. I had to consume thirty-two ounces of fluid prior to the appointment per the instructions given by my doctor. I am on the verge of peeing in my pants when the ultrasound technician finally comes out and calls me to a room.

When I get into the room the technician tells me to pull my pants down mid-thigh and lay on my back. She squirted a lukewarm gel on my lower abdomen and rolled a transducer back and forth. "I am not getting a good picture, but it looks like twins," she said. What the hell did she just say? Twins! Twins don't run in my family. Is that what the other doctor saw? He thought my other baby was a f---ing cyst or fibroid? She told me that she needed to perform a transvaginal ultrasound to get a closer view of the possible fetuses. I still have to pee; now she shoves that eight inch phallic shaped transducer inside my poor vagina. She informed me that once she got the baby or babies' heartbeat I could empty my bladder. "Look!" she exclaimed. "Do you see that one?" I looked over and saw a tiny being that resembled a lima bean with a heartbeat. Wait, what did she mean that one? Was she serious about the twin thing? "Look, here is another one," she said. What did she mean another one? So it was true I was pregnant with twi--" "Oh My God!" she exclaimed before I could finish my thought. "There is another one in here, you have triplets!" I was in total shock. After a few minutes she asked me if I wanted her to go get "him", (my fiancé). Hell yeah, go get "him" since he is the one responsible for this! She exited and quickly returned with "him." "Look, she said "there's one, there's number two, and look number three!" My fiancé looked as if he was going to faint. He excused himself and quickly went back to the waiting room to have a seat. I immediately jumped up and ran to the bathroom. When I returned, the technician told me that I was approximately seven weeks pregnant and handed over an ultrasound photograph with what appeared to be three little peas. I quickly tucked the ultrasound in my purse and went out to the lobby to meet my fiancé.

Once in the lobby my fiancé was nowhere to be found. I went outside and saw him walking across the parking lot, coming from the tobacco shop around the corner. "I had to go get a cigar," he said. "Why, did you need a cigar? Was it to celebrate the news about the babies?" I asked. "No, I needed to calm my nerves!" He exclaimed. He told me that a man in the shop told him that the triplets were going to be all girls and that his life would be over. I told him that I wouldn't mind at least one girl, since I had two sons already. Three babies at once! My mind kept racing back and forth. How are we going to take care of three babies? We left the doctor's office in disbelief.

We went to his house and my fiancé immediately got online and began looking at triplet baby strollers. He began looking at any and everything online that concerned triplets. He even found a website for parents of multiples. I was still too shocked to be excited. I was happy, but the thought of raising three babies at once was overwhelming. My fiancé asked me what I thought the sexes were going to be and told me to write them on a piece of paper. He did the same. Neither of us knew what the other wrote. He placed the pieces of paper in an envelope, sealed it, and placed them in a fire proof storage box to which he had the only key. He said that we would open the box after they were born to see who was right. I agreed.

The following Monday my doctor called and informed me that she did not handle multiple births. I felt like I was being rejected or pawned off. Here I was pregnant with three babies talking to someone I had entrusted with my most personal health care needs for years, and she was giving me the boot. As my mind was wandering about who my new obstetrician would be, she asked me if I used fertility drugs or had any fertility treatments. "Hell no," I was thinking. I just told her that I had not used any fertility aids. She responded by telling me how rare spontaneous triplets were. It was almost as if she did not believe me. Nevertheless, she told me that she was not sure where she was going to transfer my medical records, but they would contact me soon. I told my fiancé about my doctor giving me the boot and acting as if she did not believe me when I told her I did not use fertility drugs. He asked me how rare spontaneous triplets were, but I had no clue. My fiancé immediately got on computer and started surfing the internet for statistics. The numbers varied, but for the most part it was something like one set of triplets were born for every 6800 births. This information was for spontaneous births. Most couples that used fertility treatments had twins or higher order multiples.

The next day I decided to do a little research on the internet regarding factors that may increase the chances of conceiving multiples. Being thirty-five or older and just getting off oral contraceptives were mentioned. I did not really understand what age had to do with an increased risk of having multiples, but I am no medical professional. From what I understood about abruptly discontinuing oral contraceptives, your eggs can hyper ovulate. This occurs when you release more that one egg at a time during your normal ovulation period. I guess that was it. I was the only person I knew that conceived triplets, spontaneous or otherwise. I knew several people who had twins. There were a couple of sets of twins in my family, but not in the immediate family. I figured when I finally tell people the news, they will not believe it. I could hardly believe it. If not for the evidence of the ultrasound photo with my three little peas, I probably still would not believe it. It was still relatively early in the pregnancy, so I was not showing. It was amazing that three little babies were forming inside of me. The more I thought about it, the more the idea grew on me (pun intended.) I guess I can just relax and get used to the idea of being a mother of triplets, although it is still quite incredible.

The next week went by so fast I could not recall anything that transpired. On the twenty-fourth I was going about my day and all seemed well. All of a sudden I felt moisture between my legs. I started to bleed. It was heavy like a period. "I am miscarrying", I thought to myself. I immediately called my fiancé and he came over and rushed me to the hospital. I was immediately given an ultrasound and my cervix was checked by a doctor. My cervix was closed, which was a good sign. I was unable to see the monitor during the ultrasound, but the doctor told my fiancé and I that all of the babies were fine. Due to the blood loss, however, it was classified as a threatened abortion, which is the medical term for possible miscarriage. I went home to lie down as I was instructed.

I had to follow up with my doctor the next day. She told me that I needed to be on bed rest for a few days. She also decided to give me a breast exam, since I couldn't remember the last time (never) I had given myself one. She checked the left breast without incident and proceeded to check the right one. She felt and prodded then gave me a strange look. "You have a lump." I have a lump? She told me she wanted me to see a specialist and gave me a referral. I called my mom and fiancé and told them the news about my breast. I decided not to worry until I had a prognosis.

I made an appointment for the twenty-seventh too see about my breast. The doctor felt around my right breast for a few minutes and confirmed that there was indeed a lump there. He scheduled my lumpectomy for May fifth. I was very concerned about the procedure because I knew I had to be administered a general or local anesthetic. I didn't know what effect that would have on the babies. I called my former OB/GYN as soon as I got home from the appointment and told her my concerns. She said that as long as I got local anesthesia the babies would be fine. Even though she was no longer my doctor, technically, she was still working in concert with the breast specialist, since she was the one who discovered the lump. I was scheduled for an ultrasound on my breast the next day. He told me that I was unable to get a mammogram due to the pregnancy. The doctor said that if the findings of the ultrasound were favorable, I may not need the lumpectomy. Whew, a weight lifted off me. I guess now all I have to worry about is what the results of the ultrasound are going to be.

In the meantime, even though I was not sure what the prognosis was going to be regarding my breast, I decided to tell my mom about the babies. "Mom, guess what," I started. "What?" She questioned. "I'm pregnant." "Okay." She said. "Mom, it gets better." I said. "Is it twins?" Better I said. "What are you talking about?" She said. "I am going to have triplets!" I exclaimed. "You are kidding", she said. "No ma'am I am serious", I concluded. She said she needed to call me back (I guess she was in shock) and we hung up.

It was April twenty-eight and I had to get ready for my ultrasound appointment. I was nervous, but I had to get this over with so I could continue to bask in the glow of pregnancy. I had to get the ultrasound done at the hospital across the street from the doctor's office. I figured if something was wrong, he could come right over and cut off my cancerous boob. I was called to ultrasound and headed back for what could determine whether or not I needed a uni-bra. The ultrasound technician squirted that gel I am used to getting squeezed on my stomach, onto my right breast. She moved the transducer in a circular motion several times around my breast. She did not say anything at first, and then asked me if I had a history of breast cancer in my family. I did not think this was a good thing. On top of that she made sure not to let me see the monitor as she was scanning. Not that I would have known what I was looking for, but it just seemed bad. After she was done, she told me she needed to get another technician to look at her findings, then a doctor. She told me that my doctor would contact me regarding the results in the next few days. I assumed that this was also bad.

On the twenty-ninth my fiancé and I decided to spend some quality time together. We had been given a barrage of shocking news in the first quarter of this month. As we lay in the bed, I began feeling a little crampy. I got up and went to the bathroom. I hesitated briefly, and then wiped myself anticipating the worst. I quickly looked at the tissue to ensure that there were no surprises. Luckily, there was no blood and I went to bed peacefully.

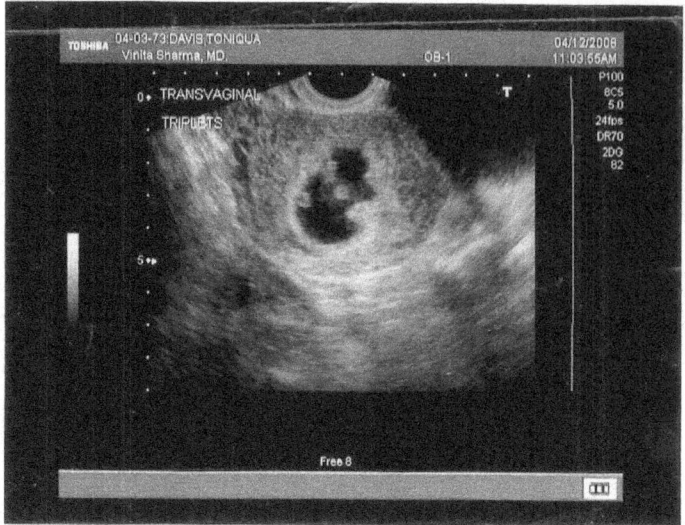

Chapter Four
May-Another Scare

It was May second. I received a call from my doctor and he confirmed the news about my ultrasound results. Based on the ultrasound, the lump looked as if it may be cancerous. The only way to determine whether it malignant or not was to perform the lumpectomy. The doctor informed me that this did not mean that it was definitely cancer. He said to just wait until after the lumpectomy and be guided by the results then. He told me to relax for the next couple of days and prepare for the fifth. That was easy for him to say. I told my mom and my fiancé the news. They were both not happy to hear the latest findings. I assured both of them that I would be fine (although I did not believe that myself.) I took a deep breath and relaxed as best I could and prepared for the fifth as I was instructed.

May fifth is here and I am preparing for my lumpectomy. Ironically, this is the anniversary of my Nana's birthday. She passed away almost nine years ago. I am not in the best of sprits because of the nature of my appointment as well as the fact that I still grieve for my Nana at times. I am sure the outcome will be positive. My mother and fiancé are both here to support me, so I should be okay. I waited for approximately an hour before the doctor was ready to perform the surgery. Once inside the operating room, a cold brown liquid, which I believe was Betadine, was rubbed all over my right breast. Then the doctor produced a very long needle and injected different areas of my right breast and under my right arm with the local anesthetic. After he confirmed that my breast was numb, the doctor began an incision around my nipple. Although it was supposed to be numb I felt some pain. As a matter of fact, I felt every pull, tug, poke, and prod until the procedure was over. After surgery, my breast was wrapped and bandaged. I also had to wear a support bra for three days. I had to change the dressing on my breast and monitor it for fluid leakage. At least the worst part was over. Now all I had to do was wait for the results.

So many thoughts flooded my mind in the days following the surgery. I wondered about if the results came back malignant, was I going to be able to have my babies? If I were continue the pregnancy how long would I live afterward? Would any of the treatment I may need have an adverse effect on the babies? I finally decided to stop thinking so much and continue functioning as a normal person that may have cancer carrying triplets. As the days flew by, my fears and concerns regarding the babies and possibly having cancer grew. I tried not to worry, but I could not help myself. I knew it was a waiting game, so I convinced myself that all I could do was wait. The weeks came and went, but my fears remained constant. I really tried not to worry so much, but it was extremely hard.

I decided to use this time waiting for the results, to break the news about the triplets to the kids and other family members. The kids sided with the doctor and agreed that I was too old for one baby, let alone three. The other members of my family all had a general sense of shock and disbelief. Overall, I think the news went over well. I made sure not to mention the possible cancer diagnosis. It just seemed like it would be too much too digest at once. The days were slowly passing by.

It was May twenty-third. I got up to use the bathroom as usual and felt drops of liquid leaking from me after I finished. I stood up, looked in the toilet, and saw blood. I was mortified. I wiped myself and saw a grape sized blood clot and more blood. I immediately started to cry. My fiancé ran into the bathroom helped me into some clothes (I was wearing pajamas), and rushed me to the hospital. I remember from the last time, one of the questions the doctor asked was did I pass any clots or tissue and I hadn't. I felt that since I did this time, a miscarriage was inevitable. I was seen by an emergency room physician and he told me the prognosis was not good. He said that my cervix was closed and he was going to send me upstairs for an ultrasound. Once upstairs, the ultrasound technician squeezed that cold gel onto my stomach and placed the transducer on top. I hesitated to look at the screen because I was afraid that one or all of the babies were dead. To my surprise, the technician squealed with delight as she showed my fiancé and I three wiggling little bodies. I was told that I was still not out of the woods yet, and to go home and rest. I followed the instructions as ordered and tried not to do anything strenuous. My stomach was noticeably round and I felt that I was a little big to be twelve weeks along. I was carrying three babies, so I figured that this must be normal and did not worry about it. I rubbed my stomach and went to sleep. My fiancé kept a close watch over me for the next few weeks.

Chapter Five
June-Triple Threat

It is June third and all is well. The results came back and the lump was benign. I was told it was a cyst, but I would have to come back in a year to monitor my breast for any changes. The doctor told me that I should also have a regular mammogram on both breast, since one could not be performed due to my pregnancy. I have been checking both breast as instructed, but they are swollen and sore, so I don't know if there are any lumps or not. I was happy to hear that I was not going to have to worry about the complications of cancer. That was a load off my back.

I am looking forward to an upcoming appointment at Maternal Fetal Medicine on the seventeenth. My doctor transferred me to their office, because she felt their office was one of the best at handling multiple births. They have to scan all of the babies to ensure they are growing properly and that they do not have any visible physical abnormalities. Initially, I was not pleased with my Maternal Fetal Medicine doctor. On my first visit, he informed me that triplet pregnancies are very risky and that a procedure called selective reduction is often utilized to eliminate the risks. The procedure involves one or more of the fetuses being injected with a solution to cause it to die. The remaining fetuses continue to grow until the time of delivery. In the meantime, the deceased fetus is being carried with the live fetuses. I was totally disgusted. Of course that was not an option. At any rate, the doctor informed me that he was not in any way suggesting that I have the procedure done, but that he had to make the option available to me. After overcoming that hurdle, I am more confident with his knowledge and expertise. I realized he was obligated to give me that information as a practitioner, but it just seemed gruesome for a doctor to make an option like that available.

Well today is the day. The seventeenth is here. We wrote the predictions for the sexes of the babies in April, but today the answer will be revealed. My fiancé and I have been going back and forth about the sexes of the babies all day. I think it is two girls and a boy. He thinks it is two boys and a girl. I know it must be a least on girl because I have been nauseous since my seventh week. We arrived to the doctor's office fifteen minutes early and still had to wait over an hour to be seen. I was just anxious to see if they were okay, because of the previous scares. Finally we were called to a room. Now comes the moment of truth.

With each ultrasound visit there is a lot of fluid intake involved and you cannot empty your bladder until after the ultrasound is almost complete. Of course I had to pee before I even sat on the table, but I had to suck it up (literally). The technician squeezed the gel on my stomach and began her scan. Her primary concern was the anatomy and whether or not there were any deformities. She checked each baby individually and labeled them Baby A, Baby B, and Baby C. Baby A was first. She checked the bladder, brain, heart, kidneys, liver, and lungs. It seemed that Baby A was doing well and was the correct size for a gestational age of sixteen weeks and two days. My fiancé and I were looking at the monitor with anticipation. She asked if we wanted to know the sex. "Yes!" we said simultaneously. I had been online doing research of my own and I knew that the female genitals of a female fetus resembled a hamburger, yes a hamburger. I looked at the monitor as she scanned near Baby A's buttocks. I saw the "hamburger" before she could even tell us it was a girl. I was ecstatic. Finally a girl, after having two boys this would be refreshing. She still had to check Babies B and C. Baby B's brain, heart, kidneys, liver, and lungs were fine, but she had to wait and re-check the bladder after she scanned Baby C. She asked if we wanted to know the sex now or when she rechecked the bladder. We wanted to know ASAP! Low and behold, another hamburger, I mean girl! I was beside myself. Baby C's bladder, brain, heart, kidneys, liver, and lungs were also fine and also she was also a girl! The man in the tobacco shop was right! Three girls! I was so excited. My fiancé just sat there with a blank expression for about five minutes, and then he looked like he was warming up to the idea. I still had to wait and see if all was well with Baby B's bladder. It turned out that her bladder had the proper function and we were free to go (and I was finally free to go to the bathroom).

Once we left the doctors office and went to my apartment, my fiancé and I started bouncing names off of each other. Because of his family tradition, all of the children's names began with the letter "D". "What about Deja?" no he said "What about Dannica?" absolutely not, I said. We went on and on for hours. We decided to go with the middle names first. We agreed on Kennedy and Kaitlyn. He wanted the third to be a form of his sister's middle name which is Kenyetta, so he decided on Kenyette. We still had plenty of time left so we did not come to an agreement on the girls' names for days.

Today is June eighteenth. I completed my paperwork for Maternity leave from work, so today was my last working day. I know it is early, but I read about complications during multiple pregnancies. Besides, I had already been through a few close calls with this pregnancy where I just so happened to be at home. I feel that if I am off now, it will decrease future risks or complications.

It was June twenty-fourth, and I received a call from Maternal Fetal Medicine regarding the ultrasound. I was worried at first because when we left, everything was fine. I was informed that although I was initially given a due date of November twenty-fifth, the doctor was planning on a cesarean delivery one month earlier. I was also informed that I had

Placenta Previa or a low lying placenta. This condition means that your placenta is lying unusually low in your uterus, next to or covering your cervix. I was informed that this may have been the culprit for the previous bleeding episodes I had. I was told that for the duration of the pregnancy that I could not have intercourse, or do any strenuous activity. I asked how this would affect the pregnancy and I was informed that the condition usually resolves itself without treatment. I was also told that normally if the condition does not resolve itself, the babies would have to be delivered by caesarean section. I told my fiancé about my diagnosis and he was relieved that it was nothing more serious, so was I.

Now that sex was out of the question, we spent more time trying to prepare for the multiple birth process. We were living in separate homes, so we figured that the best time for me to move would be at the beginning of July. I was getting big quick! It looked as if I was sixth months pregnant and I was only seventeen weeks along. We decided the first names for the girls would be Dayton and Dakota. I decided that one should be named after my mother, Damaria, a combination of her first and middle names Deborah and Marie. Now that we got the name situation figured out it was time to move on to plan B.

It was June twenty-sixth. My fiancé and I anticipated a summer wedding, however, I was getting bigger by the minute. We went to a few local chapels and got estimates. We figured that we should try to get married no later than August so that I could still be on my feet in case I had to go on bed rest. I read that sometimes with multiples, it is ordered by the doctor for the duration of the pregnancy if there are complications. I had already had my fair share of scares and I did not want to take any chances. We collected brochures from halls, chapels and churches and decided that we may try to shoot for August eighth. We even contemplated going away to get married, but we both decided that it may be too much of a risk. I was already as big as a house, but with the girls not due for a few more months we figured August to be a safe bet. I knew that the girls could possibly be born a little sooner than anticipated by the doctor, however, I assumed August was way too early. In my mind I believed that the earliest they would be born would probably be around late September or early October. Therefore, it seemed that a date in August would be ideal. With all that being said, August eighth it is for the tentative wedding date.

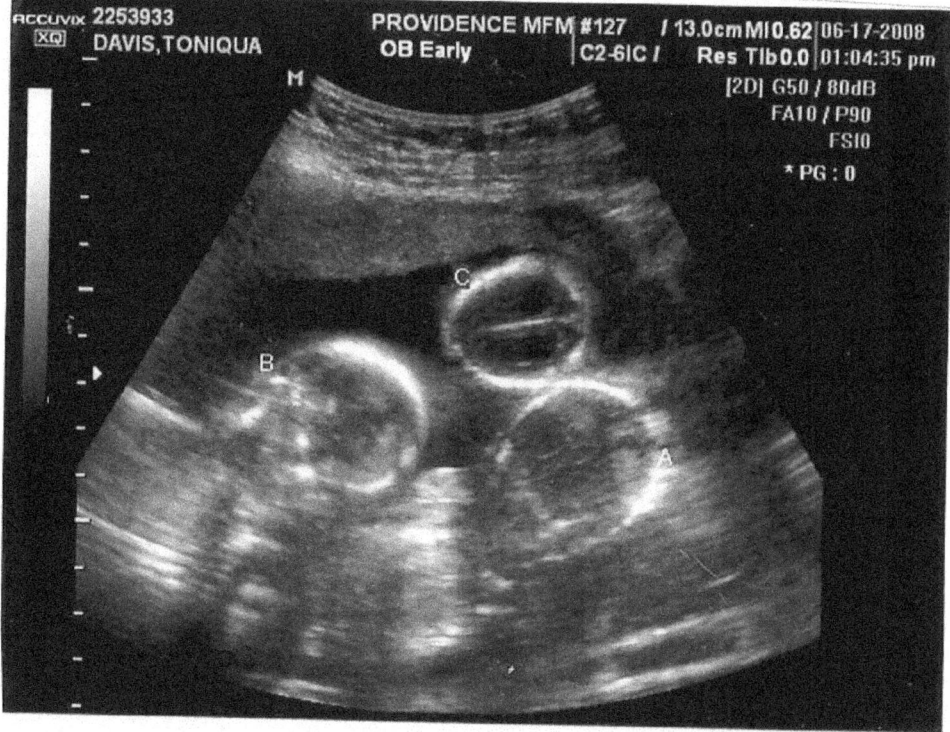

Chapter Six
July-Foreshadowing

It was July second. I was packing a few things for the move to my fiancés house. My sons were helping to pack some of my things, when all of a sudden I felt pain on my right side. It was a throbbing pain. I sat down for a while, but I kept feeling the same pain. I drove myself to the hospital and called my fiancé on the way. Once I was seen, I was hooked up to a baby heart monitor and a contraction monitor. The babies were all doing fine, but I was having contractions. I was kept overnight for observation and given a suppository (ouch!) of Indocin to stop the contractions. I was released the next day and told to stay off my feet.

I relaxed as I was ordered. My sons and my fiancé finished the packing and moving process. We moved July fifth. Moving into someone else's house is a big adjustment. Although we were planning to get married, my fiancé and I had a few disagreements about house rules. For the most part he was valid in his suggestions, but I felt we all needed a little time to adjust.

Once settled in to our new environment I started to feel a little more comfortable. I used my down time to do a little online research about triplet births and the possible complications. I was a little apprehensive to do any triplet research at first, because of the simple fact that I was considered high risk if this were a single birth. The risks I was told I may incur were now threefold. I made sure to explore all the positive and negative aspects of carrying triplets, so that I would not be biased. I wanted to be prepared for whatever complications, if any, I could possibly face with this pregnancy. I did not get into the whole online triplet frenzy until after it seemed I would have a successful pregnancy. With the previous scares, it was a little harder for me to finally let go of all of my apprehensions and feel special to be carrying multiples. I did not know where to start, so I just went to various search engines, entered "triplets", and went from there. I was not prepared for some of the things I saw.

One of the first websites I saw showed a husband and wife in a wedding photo. It went on to describe how much they desired children, but were unable to conceive. The couple went through a series of In-vitro Fertilization (IVF) treatments, and was finally successful. If I can recall correctly, three eggs were implanted into the wife's uterus and all of them survived the process. From my understanding of this, most of the time some or all of the eggs are unable to be fertilized for various reasons. The wife was able to carry the triplets, two boys, and one girl, to thirty-one weeks gestation. The babies appeared healthy, but were very tiny and had to be placed on ventilators. They were born around Christmas, so there were pictures of the babies with teeny Santa hats and each of them was inside of their own Christmas stocking. How cute! The babies all seemed to be doing well as they chronicled the following weeks. At the very end of the webpage there was a picture of the baby girl by herself. Next to her picture there was a painting of three teddy bears. Two of the teddy bears were standing in a field with blue bow ties around their necks waving goodbye to another teddy bear who was above them in a hot air balloon, wearing a pink bowtie. I read the caption underneath the painting and began bawling. Apparently, this was a memorial website for the triplet daughter the couple lost. There was no way I could tell from the way the webpage was set up in the beginning. The baby girl died as a result of complications from her pre-maturity. Both of her brothers survived. I was devastated. My doctor informed me that it was very possible that my babies would be premature, but I never imagined that one on them could possibly die as a result. I decided that it was not in my best interest to do anymore research that day.

The next day I figured that I would start anew. I braved the internet once again, this time filtering my search. I read a story about a woman who delivered full term triplets, all girls. The babies did not suffer any complications, however, the mother did. She underwent a caesarean, which is usually the standard for multiple births. During the birthing process she lost an enormous amount of blood. She had to receive a blood transfusion and was administered a total of six units of blood. She went into shock and had to be resuscitated. She was eventually stabilized, however, the babies were released from the hospital before she was. The thought that I could possibly die during the birth of my triplets never occurred to me. That was not even discussed by my doctor. He was sure to go over all the complications that the babies could suffer, but he never mentioned that something bad could happen to me. I decided to stay off the internet for the time being. My fiancé agreed. I was driving him crazy with all the information I uncovered while doing my online research.

The following day I did as I was instructed by my doctor. I relaxed. I did not get on the internet, wash clothes, wash dishes, cook dinner, or do anything that involved standing (except go to the bathroom). I continued to rest for the next week. I continued to get bigger and bigger. I was only eighteen weeks pregnant, but I looked like I was eight months along. During my previous online research I looked up pictures of women carrying triplets. I looked relatively larger than the other mothers carrying triplets. However, I just chalked it up to the fact that all women carry their babies differently, and did not worry about it. All seemed to be going well until....

It is July seventeenth, exactly one month from the day we found out about our girls. I was admitted to the hospital for pre-term labor. I was petrified. I was told at twenty-one weeks, there is nothing done to save an infant delivered that early. I was given another dose of Indocin, given an I.V, and monitored. My labor stopped, but I had to be admitted. My fiancé spent every night at the hospital with me and it helped ease my mind a little. On day five the doctor came into my room and delivered some shocking news. He said that two of the triplets, babies A and B, developed a condition called Twin to Twin Transfusion Syndrome (TTTS). He said that without treatment the result is always fetal death of one or both of the affected babies. He suggested selective reduction again. How the hell did he expect me to pick one of my children that I feel growing inside of me, that I named, to kill! What an ass, I thought. Instead of calling him any of the names I had on the tip of my tounge, I asked him what the options for treatment were, besides murdering one of them. He told me that serial amniocentesis was an option, where amniotic fluid is drained from the baby with the most fluid. He also suggested laser surgery to separate the placenta. I was ready to try anything to save the lives of our babies. On day six I was given another ultrasound and told that the fluid looked "better" around Baby B and that I may be released the next day. It is July twenty-fourth, day seven. I was finally released from the hospital. I was told that I had to have weekly ultrasounds to monitor the TTTS, but I was happy to be free. That last thing I was told was that the fluid appeared to be under control and to keep my weekly ultrasound appointments.

It was good to be home. My fiancé was going out of town on business on the twenty-fifth, so I only had a day to spend with him. We spent the evening together laughing and talking. The next morning I had to get up early so we could get to the airport by six o'clock in the morning. On the way to the airport, he told me he was going to paint the nursery pink as soon as he got back. I told him that would be a good idea. He gave me a kiss and waved goodbye, as he walked to his terminal. I drove home and laid down for a while. My stomach looked as if I was nine months pregnant, but I was only twenty two-weeks.

Against my better judgment (and my fiancés wishes), when I awoke from my nap, I decided to go online and try to find out more information about TTTS. From what I read, the treatment options available were what the doctor informed me about when I was in the hospital. When I was released, I was under the impression that the situation had resolved itself. I just wanted a little more information in case the disorder returned. I also wanted to be more educated in regard to the condition overall. Most of the treatment was successful if done at the right time by the right practitioner. I did not feel that I would need these services. I just wanted to be informed. After reading about a few instances where one or all of the babies died as a result of the disorder or the procedure I logged off of the computer. I was done scaring the shit out of myself for the day. The doctor had already done an excellent job at it.

The next day was quite uneventful. My fiancé called and said he left some items behind that he needed for his trip. I had my son go retrieve the items, because I was still taking it easy. I dropped the items off at the post office and came home to lie down on the couch. It was so hot. I woke up and felt moisture between my legs. I looked at the couch and saw a small quarter-sized stain. It was clear and did not have an odor. I went to the bathroom and sat back on the couch. I stood up and again there was a small stain, but this time it was the size of a dime. I called my friend who lives ten minutes away to tell her what was going on. She said she would take me to the hospital, but she was not home at the time. I went upstairs, got in the shower, and waited for my friend. I called my fiancé to tell him what was happening that I was going to the hospital. He called my cousin and told her to meet me there.

My friend came and picked me up. On the way to hospital we talked about baby shower ideas. I told her that I did not want to make any plans until I was at least six months pregnant. I did not anticipate anything going wrong, I just heard that it is bad luck to buy things for a baby prior to three months before it is born. We arrived to the hospital at approximately six thirty in the evening. I was placed on a monitor and given an I.V. I was told I was having contractions, but I was not given any Indocin to stop them this time. I did not feel the contractions at this time. They checked the babies' heartbeats, and they were all fine. My friend had an appointment to make, so I told her to go ahead and that my cousin would be meeting me. The nurse came into the observation room and told me that I would be admitted overnight for observation. I asked her if they could check and see if I was leaking fluid. A doctor came in with a swab and told me that if the swab turned blue it was amniotic fluid, and if it did not turn blue, it was nothing to worry about. The swab did not turn blue, so my mind was at ease. While waiting for a room, my cousin came and checked my condition. I told her what they said, and she said she would stay with me until I was checked into my room.

At around ten o'clock in the evening I was given my room. I asked my cousin to contact my fiancé and keep him abreast of the situation. I didn't feel any contractions, but the monitor indicated otherwise. I told my cousin to go home and that I would call her in the morning when I was ready to go home. She stayed for another hour then went home. At around midnight, I pushed the call button for the nurse. I was starting to feel the contractions. She gave me morphine for the pain and told me that I could not be given any medication to stop the labor, since I was there a week ago. I was given a bed pan just in case I had to use the bathroom. They wanted me to be confined to my bed. I called my fiancé soon thereafter, and told him what was going on. He asked me if he needed to come home. I told him I didn't think so, because I was under the impression that I would be going home tomorrow. I finally dozed off at about twelve thirty.

At three o'clock in the morning I sat up in the bed like a bolt of lightning struck me. I felt a rush of warm liquid gushing from between my legs. I knew immediately that my water had broken. I paged the nurse and began screaming and crying. I called my fiancé and told him he had better get back here now. I was so hysterical the nurse took the phone from me and told him what was going on. "**It's too soon**," I screamed!" The nurse told me to relax and not to worry unless I was dilated. A doctor came into the room and checked my cervix. I was five centimeters dilated. The nurse went to get confirmation from another doctor on whether or not to administer steroids to develop the babies' lungs. She was told that I was not going to be given the steroid because I was only twenty-two weeks along. I was in so much pain. The doctor went and got a portable ultrasound to monitor the babies' heartbeats at around eight o'clock in the morning. Baby A did not have a heartbeat. One of my babies was dead. Babies B and C were still active and had heartbeats. Only one of the sacs ruptured. I was still in active labor. I asked the doctor if he could save my other babies. He did not respond. An epidural was administered at noon. My fiancé was back in town and at the hospital by then. My mother, aunt and cousin had also arrived. My mother had just had surgery a week prior, so she was in a wheel chair. At around two in the afternoon the doctor came in with an announcement.

The news would prove to be devastating.

The doctor announced that Baby A was deceased and that she was lodged in my birth canal. He added that at twenty-two weeks gestation, the prognosis for the other babies was grim. He said even if they were born breathing, life saving procedures were only performed on babies that were at least twenty-four weeks. He was basically saying that my babies could come out walking, and they would do nothing to save them if they somehow lost the ability to breathe on their own. I was numb. I was laying there knowing one of my babies was dead, and now the doctor was saying the other two had death sentences. My babies were two weeks shy of being able to receive life saving treatment. No one said anything until after he left the room. My mother kissed my stomach and said goodbye to the girls, (these would have been her only granddaughters). My fiancé did not say a word. I think he believed somehow at least one of our babies would survive. I wished I could be that optimistic. I felt Babies' B and C moving around inside of me. I took it as a sign of hope, but I knew it would take a miracle for one of our babies to survive.

It was around four o'clock in the afternoon when the pain started up again. Even with the epidural I could still feel the contractions. They were strong. My mother, aunt and cousin left the room. My father and step-mother arrived. I told them the news and they sat there stunned. At around five o'clock in the evening I felt an enormous amount of pressure and the urge to push. The doctor came in and checked my cervix again, I was six centimeters. He said because the babies were very early pre-term, that I did not have to dilate the full ten centimeters. My step-mother and fiancé were the only ones in the room with me, when the doctor assembled two nurses and they prepped the room for delivery. I was ordered by the doctor to push, so I did. It felt like the baby was lodged in my cervix. I kept pushing and pushing and finally after about thirty minutes Baby A, Damaria Kenyette was born. She was so fragile and tiny. I looked at her hoping that the monitor and the doctor were wrong and that she was alive. She was lifeless. I was able to get a quick glance at her face and she was whisked away so that she could be cleaned up and dressed. I cried for her. My step-mother left the room and gave me and my fiancé some privacy. It was July twenty-seventh.

After she was cleaned up the nurse brought Damaria in and placed her in a clear plastic crib. She was dressed in a knit outfit with a matching cap. There was a piece of tape affixed to her top that read Baby A. I asked the nurse to bring her to me. I held her and kissed her tiny face. Her face was bruised, I guess because she was lodged in my cervix for so long. Otherwise, she was beautiful. She was my first born daughter. The nurse placed her back in the crib and I allowed my mother, cousin, aunt, and father in to see her. My mother held her. My aunt and cousin did not want to see her. I guess the thought of holding a dead baby was kind of morbid. My father and fiancé stared off in the distance. I guess men handle grief differently. Two of my cousins and the friend that dropped me off at the hospital arrived. Only my friend decided to see Damaria, but only for minute. After a few hours the nurse came to take Damaria away. I was still hanging on to the idea that Baby B and Baby C would survive. As it got later only my fiancé remained. He went home and retrieved a few items of clothing and returned around midnight. It was July twenty-eighth.

It was about two o'clock in the morning and I felt a throbbing sensation in my cervix. I told my fiancé to call the nurse. The next thing I knew, the doctor was called in and my second bag of water was ruptured, manually. It was two forty-one. Baby B, Dakota Kaitlyn was born. Seven minutes later Baby C, Dayton Kennedy was born. I did not get a chance to see them because I was rushed to surgery. Apparently there were two placentas. One of the placentas became stuck. They had to perform a D&C to remove it. I lost so much blood, I had to sign a consent form for a transfusion. Because I was semi-conscious, I could not be given any sedatives. I felt them pulling and scraping the placenta from my body. I was so numb from the delivery I almost could not feel anything. I did not hear my babies cry, so I assumed the worst. When I was wheeled back into my room it looked like a horror movie, there was blood everywhere. They immediately hooked me up to an I.V. and administered two units of blood. I asked to see my babies, but the nurse said I needed to rest. My fiancé checked to see if I was okay and went to sleep in the chair next to my bed.

First thing in the morning I asked about the girls again. They finally brought them all in together. Damaria was wearing a multicolored pastel knit sweater and pants with a yellow knit hat. Dakota was wearing a lavender and pink knit sweater and pants with a pink knit cap. She was slightly bruised like Damaria. It may have been due to the birthing process or the TTTS syndrome. Dayton was wearing a multicolored knit dress with a matching knit cap. I held Damaria again. She was wrapped in a yellow knit blanket, with the letter "A "affixed to it. I kissed both of her cheeks and handed her off to her father. I held Dakota next. She was wrapped in a white knit blanket with the letter "B" affixed to it. I rocked her from side to side, kissed her and handed her over to her father. I held Dayton last. She was wrapped in a white blanket with the letter "C" affixed to it. I stared at her little face and she was the spitting image of her father and I. She was the only one unscathed by this ordeal. She looked as if she were sleeping. I handed her to her father. We both said our goodbyes and the nurse came in and took them back to the morgue.

In the midst of everything I had to get my blood tested again to make sure my hemoglobin was okay. After the results came back, it was determined that I needed two more units of blood. I was not really concerned about my health. I was still reeling from the shock of losing all of the girls. A chaplain came and spoke to my fiancé and I. She gave us several phone numbers for support groups and counseling services. Soon thereafter, a nurse came in and spoke to us about what our options were as far as our daughter's remains. We decided to have them cremated. The same nurse returned and gave us forms to fill out for their death certificates. I fell apart. Apparently, if a deceased fetus is born at twenty weeks or less, it is considered a miscarriage. If the fetus is twenty weeks or more, it is considered a stillbirth. All of our babies were stillborn. It was all too much for me. My fiancé filled out all of the forms and spoke to the chaplain about the final arrangements. We had the option of having a private ceremony or having them cremated and letting the hospital cover the expenses. We chose the latter. I let my fiancé handle everything in regard to their final arrangements. The thought of losing and burying three babies at once was just too much for me to bear.

During this ordeal people kept calling to "check" on me. I know that it is the nature of people to want to know if you are okay, but I did not feel like talking. Friends wanted to come visit me, but I was an emotional wreck. I had not combed my hair, I had tear stains on my face, and my eyes were swollen from crying. I had to stay in the hospital for an additional day, to ensure that my hemoglobin was up. Frankly, I didn't care if it was or not. All I wanted was to wake up from this horrific dream and take my babies home. After my hemoglobin was checked a second time it was considered acceptable. I had to stay in the hospital a few more hours for observation. I watched television and talked to my fiancé about the possibility of having a life together without a child in common. He did not want to discuss anything that was baby related at the time, and I can't say I blamed him. I was going through so many emotions, I did not know how to act or what to say. The doctor that delivered Damaria (a different doctor delivered Dakota and Dayton) came in to check on me. He asked me if I planned on trying to conceive again (the taboo topic my fiancé and I were just discussing), and if we were, the ideal time period we should wait. I let my fiancé do all the talking. I did not feel like having a conversation right then. I just wanted to go home and get out of this place. Being here was a constant reminder of what transpired days ago. A nurse came in to check my vitals and soon returned with the necessary paperwork so that I could be discharged. I grabbed my clothes and had them on before she could come back with the doctor. The doctor gave me the green light and with that, I was finally released from the hell hole, I mean hospital.

I was drained, I guess that is to be expected after losing four quarts of blood and three babies. The staff gave me a few brochures that discussed child loss and they gave me three boxes, one for each of my daughters, but I was too numb to look inside. This had to be the worst day of my life. It was July thirty-first.

The next few days were equally horrible.

Chapter Seven
August-Shattered Dreams

When I got home everything hit me at once. I did not go home with babies. I went home with three separate boxes each containing the outfits the babies were wearing. I received a gold ring for each baby and a card with their names, lengths, weights, and footprints on them. Damaria weighed one pound one ounce and was eleven inches long. Dakota weighed twelve and a half ounces and was ten and a half inches long. Dayton was thirteen point six ounces and was eleven inches long. My fiancé purchased a glass picture with three butterflies from the gift shop. It was beautiful. The butterflies were positioned the way the girls were inside my womb. I sat on the floor of what was supposed to be their nursery, held the three boxes, and cried. When I finally picked myself up off the floor, I opened the closet and saw three little pink outfits my mother bought for the girls when I was about four months pregnant. I placed each box on a shelf, stacking them in order by size. I quickly took the boxes out, opened each one individually, and rubbed the tiny outfits under my nose. They smelled like the baby wash the hospital used to clean the girls up before they brought them into us so we could say our goodbyes. I held each tiny outfit out in front of me and realized they were small enough to fit a tiny doll. After my sentimental outburst, I repacked and restacked the boxes, placing them back in the closet on the shelf. I spent the rest of the day trying to stay busy so I wouldn't think about the events of last week.

The next day, my fiancé and I went to an arts and craft store to purchase items to make a scrapbook for the girls. I felt this would be therapeutic. We purchased various themes, letters, numbers, and shapes. I gathered all of the ultrasound photos and started the book. I dedicated a page to each girl and included a poem written by my oldest son. Everything was chronological order. I also included their footprints and gold rings. The hospital took pictures of the girls singly and together. Initially, I did not want to include the pictures, but eventually I did. I wanted to remember everything about my girls. The girls I would never know.

I went through so many mixed emotions. At first I was very sad. I didn't want to talk to friends, relatives, or even my fiancé. I wondered what I did to "deserve" this. I thought that there were so many times we thought we were going to lose the girls and we didn't. Why did we lose them when we didn't expect it? Why was I allowed to come this far along in the pregnancy to lose them all? I was thinking the hospital should have or could have done more. I became an internet fanatic. I looked at support groups, but they did not seem to meet my need for immediate comfort. I became obsessed with finding cases of babies born at twenty-two weeks that survived. The cases were few are far between, but I was able to find four documented cases. Three of them were in the United States. All of them occurred before the births of my daughters. After being online for hours on end my fiancé told me to give it a break. I started to question the ethics of medicine. Why would they not even *try* to save our babies? Most research suggested that the earliest possible gestational age to successfully save an infant is twenty-four weeks. However, the infant would be very likely to have life long debilitating defects. The hospital informed me that they did not have a neonatal facility equipped to deal with the needs of very early pre-term infants. They added that even if they did, they would not provide my babies with the optimal care because of their gestational age. Deep down I knew that they were too young to survive outside of the womb, but I just wanted them to be given a chance.

It was August sixteenth. My fiancé and I decided that we needed to get away. We went to a quaint little city in our area and stayed at an inn by the water. I was nice to get away, but I kept thinking about the girls. We talked and spent quality time together. We went to a restaurant by the water, had a few drinks, and enjoyed the evening. We were still planning to get married, despite last month's tragedy. We spent the next day walking on the beach and relaxing. This may have been the first day I didn't immerse myself in thoughts about the girls. I think I am too numb too cry anymore. My sadness comes and goes. I know I must find a way to get over the pain and start healing.

Once we were back at the house I started writing poems about the girls. Poetry is a way for me to release some of my innermost thoughts and emotions. I began writing and came up with two poems for them:

Three Little Angels

One day I told God I wanted a daughter and he heard my prayer

My body subtly started to change and I knew that you were there

I went to the doctor to confirm this gift God bestowed on me

Imagine my surprise to find, not one, not two, but three

At first I was in shock, but soon I realized

God picked me to carry three, a wonderful surprise

Your dad was there and we both shared the joy of you from the start

Although you were so tiny, you held a huge place in our hearts

As the weeks flew, my tummy grew

And so did all of you

We anxiously awaited October so you could make your big debut

It was a Saturday in July when I went to the hospital as I had times before

Little did I know what this visit had in store

Early Sunday morning, I started to contract

But it was way too early, three months to be exact

My dear Damaria you were first to earn your wings

To have you here a minute more, I would have given anything

The next morning your sisters Dakota and Dayton must have wondered where you went

In their quest to find out where you were, they started their ascent

Though you were here for a moment we had no chance to say hello

God needed three new angels, so we had to let you go

Although you are not here with us we will think of you each day

Three angels looking down on us Damaria, Dakota, and Dayton Roche'

If I Could Only Hold You

If only I could hold you things would be okay

I often think of how I felt, losing you that day

If I could only hold you I would feel complete

I kiss you from your forehead to the bottoms of your feet

If I could only hold you I would cry no more

But when I lost my three angles, it shocked me to the core

If I could only hold you I know exactly what I would say

I would tell you mommy loves you each and every day

If I could only hold you I would give you my all

You were born this summer, though you were not due 'til fall.

The pain of losing you is endless, but I will see you again

When I make my way to heaven, I will hold you then

After writing I felt a little better. It did not take my mind off of things completely, but it was a start. My fiancé and I still have to figure out when and where we are getting married. The loss of the girls, threw us for a loop, but somehow we managed to stay strong for each other.

I decided that I needed to keep myself busy, so I started doing various projects around the house. I began with basic things like shampooing the carpet and the furniture. Then I decided to paint the bathroom. After I painted, the walls still seemed a little dull. I decided to apply paintable wallpaper and I painted that too. I purchased several home improvement books to get more ideas. My fiancé thought I needed to take a break from the home projects. I figured the next best thing for me to do to get back into the swing of things and to keep my mind occupied was to return to work. I knew that I was not prepared for the discussion about what happened with the girls, but I knew I had to go back eventually. Now was just a good a time as any.

On August twenty-fourth, I went online (not to look up anything about babies) to look up possible wedding venues. Despite everything, my fiancé and I were still planning to get married. Initially, I wanted a dress, guest, and a small ceremony. After the recent events, neither one of us felt like a ceremony, so we decided to get "hitched" at the city hall. The ceremonies were only performed on Fridays. The upcoming Friday and following Friday were booked. The next available date was September twelfth. I called my fiancé and asked him what he thought of that date, he said it was fine, and it was booked. It was not the lavish wedding that most women dream of, but I was marrying the man I loved and that is all that mattered.

On August twenty-sixth, I called my boss and told her to expect me back sometime next month. She asked me if I had a definite date, so I opted for the eighth. I figured the more I sat at home, the more I would dwell on the loss of my babies. It seemed as if it were a bad dream sometimes. Then it would replay in my mind over and over. I kept thinking to myself, was there anything I could have done to prevent this from happening? I needed to do something to keep the events that transpired on July twenty-seventh and twenty-eighth from controlling my life. These dates will be forever etched in my mind. I knew it would be very difficult, but I had to find the strength to move forward and get past this. My fiancé did not talk about it much. I am sure he dealt with it in his own way. He was already back to work. In fact, he was back to work a week after I came home from the hospital. I needed more time to get myself together and make sense of all this before I was ready to face the outside world again. I only had a week to prepare for my journey back into the real world. My life before I lost my daughters.

Chapter Eight
September-Leave Me the F—k Alone
(Back to Work)

Today is the eighth day of September. This is my first day back to work. I sure hope that everyone does not start crowding into my office asking me a bunch of damn questions. The office where I work is owned by the city, but shared by several entities. The division where I worked knew about what happened with the girls. Some of the employees that worked in the adjoining offices had no idea. This led to a bit of awkwardness and confusion. People were asking to see pictures of the babies. I had pictures, but I am quite sure if I would have whipped out the post mortem photographs of the girls, they may have sent me to a psychiatric ward. I had to address each unknowing soul and fill them in on the tragic events. This was unexpected, but understandable. I know those people felt just as awkward after asking me about the girls as I did explaining it.

On the other hand, there were those who knew exactly what happened and were still ignorant enough to ask some outlandish questions. Luckily, I am generally mild mannered and easy going (unless I am pushed.) My office mate is very outspoken, so when people came into our office with dumb shit, she ushered them away, without saying a word. She could look at someone and they would know to shut the f—k up instantly. I understand that some people just don't know what to say. Most of my co-workers were sympathetic and did not question me much. Some of the asses that I work with felt the need to ask the most invasive, insensitive questions. People asked me questions like:

Were the babies really little? Did they look like you or your fiancé? How do you feel after your miscarriage? You are not going to try again are you? Do you have pictures? My all time favorite one: Do you know how much child support you could have gotten if he would have tried to leave you?

What did they expect me to say? I feel great after my miscarriage. By the way it was not a miscarriage I delivered three dead babies you insensitive jerk! Let me get a permission slip from you the next time me and my fiancé decide to have sex and possibly make a baby!

Some of the annoying things said were comments like:

Three babies were too many anyway. This might be a blessing. You can always try again. At least you don't have to worry about day care.

I wanted all of my babies, duh. A blessing, are you kidding me. You are right I can try again, but I wanted the babies that were there in the first place you ass!

What the **F—K!**

I sat in my office working very diligently to avoid ignorance. After getting over the first few hurdles, it seems like being back to work was actually helping me cope with the loss better. I had the occasional "Girl, how you feeling today?" but other than that I was fine.

While I was off work recovering from the delivery and the aftermath, my co-workers purchased a gift card for me and enclosed it in a sympathy card. It was valued at over two hundred-fifty dollars and I was very grateful. I sent thank you cards to the office while I was off and personally thanked everyone one when I got back. One of my co-workers asked me what I purchased with it and how much did I spend on myself. Are you kidding me? NONE OF YOUR F---ING BUSINESS. LEAVE ME THE F—K ALONE. How is that answer for all of your questions?

I came home and told my fiancé how my day went. He told me not to let people get the best of me. That is easy for him to say. As far as I knew, nobody was saying that dumb shit to him. On the other hand, he told me that only a few people asked how he felt about the situation and that everyone asked him how I was doing. It did not even occur to me that people were ignoring his feelings about the loss of the girls. I guess it is just human nature to be more concerned about the mother. He was not showing a lot of emotion, so I thought he was just coping with it better than I was. I did not think that he may be just bottling it up inside. I asked him how he felt, but he simply said that he was "dealing with it." We talked a little more and I told him some of the things I thought about saying in response to some of my co-worker's questions. He advised against it. I agreed.

Today is September twelfth. This is the day my fiancé and I finally got married. We went to the local city hall and honeymooned in Niagara Falls. We had a good time, even though it rained most of the weekend. We finally got hitched. Now I can stop saying my man or my fiancé. Now I have a husband. Hopefully the loss of the girls won't put a damper on our marriage. We will see.

We arrived back to the states on September fourteenth. My husband (he he he, I'm married), asked me if I had heard anything about the memorial service for the girls. I told him I would call the hospital and follow up. I called the number the hospital provided and was routed to a voicemail box. I left a message and told my husband about the phone call. He said that if I did not hear anything in the next few days that he would drive to the hospital and speak to someone in person. I told him that we should give it some time before we took that approach. We sat on the couch and I laid in his arms for a few hours without saying a word. He still has not looked at the scrapbook I made for the girls. He said he would look at it in his own time. I guess he needs his space to come to grips with our loss. I know it is not just my loss, but it just feels like it sometimes. I was so used to feeling them moving around inside of me. Hell, my milk just dried up last month! We will get through this together. I figure once the memorial service is over, we will have a little more closure.

Today is September fifteenth. I received a call from the hospital in regard to the memorial service for the girls. Since we opted to have the hospital cover the cost of the cremation, the memorial service was a group service to be held in October. I was a little apprehensive at first, because even though I initially agreed to the group service, now I thought we should have a private service. Then I thought about how emotional it would be for the family and how long it took me to get to a point where I could discuss the girls without breaking down. I was given the number to the hospital chaplain to confirm the date.

I told my husband about the arrangements and told him it was scheduled for October the eighteenth. I asked him how he felt about everything, but he is so private with his thoughts in regard to the girls. I guess I can respect that. He did not answer my question. He said "isn't the eighteenth Sweetest Day?" I replied "yes." I guess we were both thinking the same thing. This date was just one week shy of when the doctor wanted to perform a pre-scheduled caesarean to deliver the girls. Now the service to memorialize their deaths was scheduled to be held on October eighteenth, Sweetest Day. Bittersweet.

Chapter Nine
October-Bitter Sweetest Day

Today is October eighteenth, the day of the memorial service. I was fine at first, and then a flood of emotions ran through me. This day was supposed to mean closure, but I started to feel an uneasiness that I have not felt since the day I left the hospital. I slowly gathered the suit I was going to wear and moved in slow motion after taking my shower. It took me thirty minutes to finally put my clothes on. My husband seemed to look as if he was more at peace with this situation than I was. We still have not really addressed each others emotions, but we have communicated back and forth about how we felt on certain days. Nevertheless, we had to be prepared for this day whether we were ready or not. After we were all ready, my kids, my husband, and I, all made the trek to the cemetery. It only took us twenty minutes to get there, but it seemed like we were driving for hours. Once we arrived I felt a knot in my throat. I swallowed, exited the car and stood next to my husband.

The service was held outdoors by a pond near the front gate. It was cold and rainy, befitting for the occasion. I saw two other mothers walking back and forth along the pond's edge, one of them sobbing silently to herself. Since there were no pictures or bodies to view, I only invited family to the memorial service. My husband and I were holding hands, my mother was standing with my sons, and my cousin arrived shortly before the service started. I saw my dad and step-mother walking up and soon the service began. All of the mothers had to write their child or children's names in a book and were handed a rose and a small ceramic angel embracing a child. I received three. The service started with a song and then acknowledgement of all of the babies. There were five babies being memorialized in total, three of them were mine.

After the service we all went to eat. I had not eaten much since losing the girls. I felt a little better now that the hard part was over, saying goodbye for the last time. We all went on with our day after lunch. I guess it was a sweet day after all, knowing my little baby butterflies are safe and watching over us.

After Word

One day in August my husband, (then my fiancé) and I went to play golf. My head was not really in the game, but I struggled through it. Overhead, we saw three little butterflies flying over the course. I thought to myself there they are, our babies, letting us know they are okay. The three little butterflies circled the course, and then disappeared as quickly as they had appeared. I finished the game with a smile on my face, never letting him know why I was smiling.

www.ingramcontent.com/pod-product-compliance
Lightning Source LLC
Chambersburg PA
CBHW031226090426
42740CB00007B/728